DIAMOND I

I

Perfume
Bottles
Price Guide

**and other
Drugstore Ware**

Copyright 2000

ISBN# 0-89538-112-5

L-W Book Sales
**PO Box 69
Gas City, IN 46933**

PERFUME BOTTLE SECTION

A package to meet your requirements can no doubt be found among the wide range of sizes and styles illustrated on the following pages.

In addition to these stock items we are prepared to manufacture private mould bottles of your own design.

Illinois Glass Company

Bottles made between 1910-1925

Perfumes

MOULD C H No. 54

Size		Weight per Gross
½ oz.	C H No. 441 GGS	28 lbs.
1 oz.	C H No. 442 GGS	40 lbs.
2 oz.	C H No. 442 GGS	52 lbs.
4 oz.	C H No. 443 GGS	88 lbs.

*For Machine Made Perfume and Toilet Ware
see Pages 72 to 98 inclusive.*

MOULD C H No. 54

Size		Weight per Gross
½ oz.	C H No. 201 GGS	28 lbs.
1 oz.	C H No. 201 GGS	40 lbs.
2 oz.	C H No. 202 GGS	52 lbs.
4 oz.	C H No. 204 GGS	88 lbs.
8 oz.	C H No. 205 GGS	160 lbs.

MOULD C H No. 54

Size		Weight per Gross
½ oz.	C H No. 369 GGS	28 lbs.
1 oz.	C H No. 327 GGS	38 lbs.
2 oz.	C H No. 389 GGS	53 lbs.
4 oz.	C H No. 389 GGS	85 lbs.

Furnished also with numbers 225, 226, 382, and 390 Peg Stoppers.

Illinois Glass Company

Round and French Toilets

THE Round Toilet is a good looking, practical package that appeals alike to the manufacturers of Toilet Waters and the general public. It labels well, and is made in a range of sizes that permits its use for entire lines, when desired. It is shown here with the Sprinkler Top Finish, but is also available with Cork Finish, as illustrated on Page 84.

Available in corrugated or wood reshipping cases, plain or imprinted, if desired.

ROUND TOILETS

Mould No.	Size	Quantity per Crate	Weight per Gross
Q-22	1 oz.	3 gro.	25 lbs.
Q-45	1 oz.	5 gro.	25 lbs.
Q-15	2 oz.	3 gro.	30 lbs.
P-44	3 oz.	3 gro.	40 lbs.
Q-16	4 oz.	2 gro.	50 lbs.
2028	5 oz.	2 gro.	60 lbs.
P-51	8 oz.	1½ gro.	90 lbs.
P-45	16 oz.	1 gro.	150 lbs.
P-46	32 oz.	½ gro	250 lbs.

For hand blown perfume and toilet ware see pages 205 to 247, inclusive.

ALTHOUGH the French Toilet is generally recognized as the standard package for Lilac Water, it is one of those popular bottles whose use is not confined to any one product alone. It is widely used throughout the entire Toilet Water field. Supplied also with Square Ring Cork Finish as shown on Page 76.

Available in corrugated or wood reshipping cases, plain or imprinted, if desired.

FRENCH TOILETS

Mould No.	Size	Quantity per Crate	Weight per Gross
Q-34	2 oz.	3 gro.	40 lbs.
R-81	3 oz.	3 gro.	40 lbs.
B-50	5 oz.	2 gro.	60 lbs.
D-47	6 oz.	1½ gro.	70 lbs.
165	12 oz.	1 gro.	120 lbs.

Illinois Glass Company

Toilet Water Bottles

OBLONG FLUTED TOILETS

Mould No.	Size	Quantity per Crate	Weight per Gross
T-275	½ oz.	5 gro.	15 lbs.
728	3 oz.	2 gro.	75 lbs.
T-242	3 oz.	2 gro.	65 lbs.
P-61	3½ oz.	2 gro.	70 lbs.
976	5 oz.	1½ gro.	85 lbs.
902	6 oz.	1½ gro.	95 lbs.

CONCAVE TOILETS

Mould No.	Size	Quantity per Crate	Weight per Gross
546	1 oz.	5 gro.	25 lbs.
R-1	2 oz.	3 gro.	35 lbs.
R-2	4 oz.	2 gro.	70 lbs.

For hand blown perfume and toilet ware see pages 205 to 247, inclusive.

ROUND TOILET

Mould No.	Size	Quantity per Crate	Weight per Gross
2203	16 oz.	1 gro.	150 lbs.

TAPER FOOTED TOILETS

Mould No.	Size	Quantity per Crate	Weight per Gross
A-72	2⅛ oz.	3 gro.	55 lbs.
G-79	6 oz.	1½ gro.	70 lbs.

Toilet Water Bottles

CONCAVE FOOTED TOILET

Mould No.	Size	Quantity per Crate	Weight per Gross
A-71	2½ oz.	3 gro.	55 lbs.
A-36	3 oz.	2 gro.	55 lbs.

SCREW TOP OBLONG TOILET

Mould No.	Size	Quantity per Crate	Weight per Gross
A-48	2½ oz.	2 gro.	50 lbs.

*For hand blown perfume and toilet ware
see pages 205 to 247, inclusive.*

TAPER OVAL TOILET

Mould No.	Size	Quantity per Crate	Weight per Gross
M-49	3½ oz.	2 gro.	70 lbs.

FLAT PANELED TOILET

Mould No.	Size	Quantity per Crate	Weight per Gross
K-74	3½ oz.	2 gro.	70 lbs.

Toilet Water Bottles

CONCAVE TOILETS

Mould No.	Size	Quantity per Crate	Weight per Gross
546	1 oz.	5 gro.	25 lbs.
R-1	2 oz.	3 gro.	35 lbs.
R-2	4 oz.	2 gro.	70 lbs.

CONCAVE TOILET

Mould No.	Size	Quantity per Crate	Weight per Gross
971	4 oz.	2 gro.	70 lbs.

FRENCH TOILETS

Mould No.	Size	Quantity per Crate	Weight per Gross
Q-34	2 oz.	3 gro.	35 lbs.
R-81	3 oz.	3 gro.	40 lbs.
B-50	5 oz.	2 gro.	60 lbs.
D-47	6 oz.	1½ gro.	70 lbs.
165	12 oz.	1 gro.	120 lbs.

SQUARE CONCAVE TOILET

Mould No.	Size	Quantity per Crate	Weight per Gross
H-68	8 oz.	1½ gro.	90 lbs.

OBLONG TOILET

Mould No.	Size	Quantity per Crate	Weight per Gross
235	8 oz.	1½ gro.	90 lbs.

Paris Squares

THE Paris Square, of course, is one of the old standbys that has been popular in the toilet trade for years.

It is a plain yet distinctive bottle with excellent labeling surfaces. The wide range of sizes in which it is produced makes it possible to carry the same package style through entire lines of liquid toilet preparations.

Furnished in crates or in wood or corrugated reshipping cases, plain or printed, as preferred.

PARIS SQUARE TOILET

Mould No.	Size	Quantity per Crate	Weight per Gross
T-381	½ oz.	10 gro.	15 lbs.
T-382	1 oz.	5 gro.	18 lbs.
T-357	2 oz.	5 gro.	30 lbs.
T-358	3 oz.	3 gro.	40 lbs.
T-359	4 oz.	3 gro.	50 lbs.
T-383	6 oz.	2 gro.	70 lbs.
T-360	8 oz.	1½ gro.	90 lbs.
T-361	12 oz.	1 gro.	120 lbs.
T-362	16 oz.	1 gro.	150 lbs.
T-363	32 oz.	½ gro.	250 lbs.

*Your request for samples will have
our immediate attention.*

OBLONG FLUTED TOILET

Mould No.	Size	Quantity per Crate	Weight per Gross
T-275	½ oz.	5 gro.	15 lbs.
T-242	3 oz.	2 gro.	65 lbs.
728	3 oz.	2 gro.	75 lbs.
P-61	3½ oz.	2 gro.	70 lbs.
976	5 oz.	1½ gro.	85 lbs.
902	6 oz.	1½ gro.	95 lbs.

Toilet Water Bottles

TAPER FOOTED TOILETS

Mould No.	Size	Quantity per Crate	Weight per Gross
A-72	2⅞ oz.	3 gro.	55 lbs.
G-79	6 oz.	1½ gro.	70 lbs.

FLAT TOILET

Mould No.	Size	Quantity per Crate	Weight per Gross
G-43	3 oz.	3 gro.	45 lbs.

PARIS SQUARE TOILETS

Mould No.	Size	Quantity per Crate	Weight per Gross
K-5	½ oz.	10 gro.	15 lbs.
K-6	1 oz.	5 gro.	18 lbs.
K-7	2 oz.	5 gro.	30 lbs.
K-8	3 oz.	3 gro.	40 lbs.
A-70	4 oz.	3 gro.	50 lbs.
G-60	5 oz.	2 gro.	60 lbs.
J-38	6 oz.	2 gro.	70 lbs.
E-79	8 oz.	1½ gro.	90 lbs.
222	12 oz.	1 gro.	120 lbs.
268	16 oz.	1 gro.	150 lbs.
S-71	16 oz.	1 gro.	150 lbs.
R-89	30 oz.	½ gro.	250 lbs.

FLAT TOILETS

Mould No.	Size	Quantity per Crate	Weight per Gross
G-39	1¾ oz.	3 gro.	40 lbs.
A-35	4 oz.	3 gro.	50 lbs.
417	5½ oz.	2 gro.	70 lbs.

OBLONG TOILET

Mould No.	Size	Quantity per Crate	Weight per Gross
162	4 oz.	2 gro.	60 lbs.

Illinois Glass Company

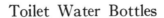

Toilet Water Bottles

OBLONG TOILET

Mould No.	Size	Quantity per Crate	Weight per Gross
D-39	8 oz.	1½ gro.	90 lbs.

TAPER OBLONG TOILET

Mould No.	Size	Quantity per Crate	Weight per Gross
Q-36	2 oz.	3 gro.	55 lbs.
F-74	4 oz.	3 gro.	50 lbs.

MINNESOTA TOILET CREAM

Mould No.	Size	Quantity per Crate	Weight per Gross
F-78	6 oz.	2 gro.	70 lbs.

For hand blown perfume and toilet ware see pages 205 to 247, inclusive.

OVAL TAPER PANEL

Mould No.	Size	Quantity per Crate	Weight per Gross
S-72	2½ oz.	2 gro.	60 lbs.

DOUBLE SQUARE TOILET

Mould No.	Size	Quantity per Crate	Weight per Gross
916	3½ oz.	2 gro.	60 lbs.

Toilet Water Bottles

SQUAT OBLONG TOILETS

Mould No.	Size	Quantity per Crate	Weight per Gross
702	4 oz.	2 gro.	50 lbs.
Q-54	5 oz.	1½ gro.	70 lbs.
L-55	10 oz.	1 gro.	110 lbs.

OBLONG TOILET

Mould No.	Size	Quantity per Crate	Weight per Gross
137	4 oz.	2 gro.	50 lbs.

TALL SQUARE TOILET

Mould No.	Size	Quantity per Crate	Weight per Gross
F-20	4½ oz.	2 gro.	80 lbs.

For hand blown perfume and toilet ware see pages 205 to 247, inclusive.

OBLONG TOILETS

Mould No.	Size	Quantity per Crate	Weight per Gross
P-10	2 oz.	3 gro.	35 lbs.
P-11	4 oz.	2 gro.	50 lbs.
S-9	12 oz.	1 gro.	120 lbs.

OBLONG TOILET

Mould No.	Size	Quantity per Crate	Weight per Gross
Rx-681	4 oz.	2 gro.	65 lbs.

Gothic Toilet Creams and Velva Toilets

THE Gothic Toilet Cream is a sturdy, good looking bottle, recognized as the standard package for Toilet Creams by both the manufacturers of toilet preparations and the general public.

Its broad panels permit varied and attractive labeling; while its semi-wide mouth allows a steady unimpeded flow of its contents when pouring.

"Diamond I" Gothic Toilets are available in reshipping cases, if desired.

A three panel bottle with the exception of D-5 which has one panel only.

GOTHIC TOILET CREAM

Mould No.	Size	Quantity per Crate	Weight per Gross
D-7	2½ oz.	3 gro.	50 lbs.
D-5	4 oz.	2 gro.	75 lbs.
918	4 oz.	2 gro.	75 lbs.

Samples gladly furnished on request.

VELVA TOILETS

Mould No.	Size	Quantity per Crate	Weight per Gross
X-1	1 oz.	5 gro.	18 lbs.
X-2	2 oz.	3 gro.	30 lbs.
X-3	3 oz.	3 gro.	40 lbs.
X-4	4 oz.	3 gro.	50 lbs.
X-6	6 oz.	2 gro.	70 lbs.
X-278	7 oz.	1½ gro.	85 lbs.
X-8	8 oz.	1½ gro.	90 lbs.
X-9	10 oz.	1 gro.	110 lbs.
X-12	12 oz.	1 gro.	120 lbs.
X-27	14 oz.	1 gro.	140 lbs.
X-16	16 oz.	1 gro.	150 lbs.

Toilet Cream Panels

TOILET CREAM PANEL

Mould No.	Size	Quantity per Crate	Weight per Gross
T-313	½ oz.	5 gro.	18 lbs.
T-302	1¼ oz.	3 gro.	40 lbs.
T-314	2 oz.	3 gro.	40 lbs.
T-311	5 oz.	2 gro.	75 lbs.

One side paneled

RUBIFOAM

Mould No.	Size	Quantity per Crate	Weight per Gross
M-95	2 oz.	3 gro.	45 lbs.

One side paneled

TOILET CREAM PANEL

Mould No.	Size	Quantity per Crate	Weight per Gross
C-63	2¾ oz.	3 gro.	45 lbs.

A one panel bottle

For hand blown perfume and toilet ware see pages 205 to 247, inclusive.

TOILET CREAM PANEL

Mould No.	Size	Quantity per Crate	Weight per Gross
947	4 oz.	2 gro.	75 lbs.

One side paneled

TOILET CREAM PANEL

Mould No.	Size	Quantity per Crate	Weight per Gross
770	3 oz.	3 gro.	45 lbs.

A one panel bottle

Toilet Water Bottles

OBLONG PANELED SHAMPOOS

Mould No.	Size	Quantity per Crate	Weight per Gross
P-62	2 oz.	3 gro.	55 lbs.
F-75	6 oz.	1½ gro.	80 lbs.
T-282	6 oz.	1½ gro.	95 lbs

A two panel bottle

PANELED OBLONG TOILET

Mould No.	Size	Quantity per Crate	Weight per Gross
G-74	6 oz.	1½ gro.	90 lbs.

A three sided panel

ROYAL OBLONG TOILETS

Mould No.	Size	Quantity per Crate	Weight per Gross
T-261	1 oz.	5 gro.	18 lbs.
E-47	3 oz.	3 gro.	40 lbs.
E-48	4 oz.	3 gro.	50 lbs.
401	6 oz.	2 gro.	70 lbs.
402	12 oz.	1 gro.	120 lbs.
T-262	16 oz.	1 gro.	150 lbs.
P-59	32 oz.	½ gro.	250 lbs.

OBLONG TOILET

Mould No.	Size	Quantity per Crate	Weight per Gross
2061	3 oz.	3 gro.	50 lbs.

OVAL PANEL TOILET

Mould No.	Size	Quantity per Crate	Weight per Gross
M-40	1¼ oz.	3 gro.	40 lbs.

A one sided panel

Toilet Water Bottles

ROUND TOILETS

Mould No.	Size	Quantity per Crate	Weight per Gross
A-69	3½ oz.	3 gro.	45 lbs.
C-90	5 oz.	2 gro.	60 lbs.
152	8 oz.	1½ gro.	90 lbs.
S-6	11 oz.	⅔ gro.	150 lbs.

CASCADE TOILETS

Mould No.	Size	Quantity per Crate	Weight per Gross
T-344	6 oz.	1½ gro.	85 lbs.
2202	8 oz.	1½ gro.	100 lbs.

ROUND TOILETS

Mould No.	Size	Quantity per Crate	Weight per Gross
Q-22	1 oz.	3 gro.	25 lbs.
Q-45	1 oz.	5 gro.	25 lbs.
Q-15	2 oz.	3 gro.	30 lbs.
P-44	3 oz.	3 gro.	40 lbs.
Q-16	4 oz.	2 gro.	50 lbs.
2028	5 oz.	2 gro.	60 lbs.
P-51	8 oz.	1½ gro.	90 lbs.
P-45	16 oz.	1 gro.	150 lbs.
P-46	32 oz.	½ gro.	250 lbs.

ROUND TOILETS

Mould No.	Size	Quantity per Crate	Weight per Gross
S-39	4 oz.	2 gro.	50 lbs.
M-65	6 oz.	1½ gro.	70 lbs.
L-1	8 oz.	1½ gro.	90 lbs.

ROUND TOILETS

Mould No.	Size	Quantity per Crate	Weight per Gross
R-37	3 oz.	3 gro.	40 lbs.

Toilet Water Bottles

RIBBED OBLONG TOILETS

Mould No.	Size	Quantity per Crate	Weight per Gross
T-296	1 oz.	3 gro.	35 lbs.
T-297	4 oz.	2 gro.	70 lbs.

TALL OBLONG TOILET

Mould No.	Size	Quantity per Crate	Weight per Gross
T-316	4 oz.	2 gro.	70 lbs.

TAPER SQUARE TOILET

Mould No.	Size	Quantity per Crate	Weight per Gross
P-72	3½ oz.	2 gro.	60 lbs.

For hand blown perfume and toilet ware see pages 205 to 247, inclusive.

TAPER OBLONG TOILETS

Mould No.	Size	Quantity per Crate	Weight per Gross
C-18	4 oz.	2 gro.	50 lbs.
H-86	8 oz.	1½ gro.	90 lbs.
I-46	16 oz.	½ gro.	215 lbs.

PYRAMID TOILETS

Mould No.	Size	Quantity per Crate	Weight per Gross
G-49	2 oz.	3 gro.	35 lbs.
658	4 oz.	2 gro.	50 lbs.

Toilet Water Bottles

FANCY TOILET

Mould No.	Size	Quantity per Crate	Weight per Gross
P-5	2 oz.	2 gro.	70 lbs.

DECORATED TOILET

Mould No.	Size	Quantity per Crate	Weight per Gross
T-342	2 oz.	2 gro.	70 lbs.

FLORIDA WATER

Mould No.	Size	Quantity per Crate	Weight per Gross
B-87	2 oz.	5 gro.	30 lbs.

For hand blown perfume and toilet ware see pages 205 to 247, inclusive.

TALL TAPER TOILET

Mould No.	Size	Quantity per Crate	Weight per Gross
H-63	2 oz.	3 gro.	45 lbs.

FLAT TAPER TOILET

Mould No.	Size	Quantity per Crate	Weight per Gross
G-97	3 oz.	2 gro.	60 lbs.

Toilet Water Bottles

PYRAMID HEXAGON TOILET

Mould No.	Size	Quantity per Crate	Weight per Gross
T-205	4 oz.	3 gro.	50 lbs

TAPER CONCAVE TOILETS

Mould No.	Size	Quantity per Crate	Weight per Gross
P-66	½ oz	7 gro	15 lbs.
M-46	1 oz.	5 gro.	18 lbs.
T-216	2 oz.	3 gro.	45 lbs.
T-186	3½ oz.	2 gro.	45 lbs.

LILY TOILETS

Mould No.	Size	Quantity per Crate	Weight per Gross
P-75	½ oz.	7 gro.	20 lbs.
J-64	1¼ oz.	3 gro.	35 lbs.
G-50	3½ oz.	1½ gro.	70 lbs.

For hand blown perfume and toilet ware see pages 205 to 247, inclusive.

HEXAGON TOILET

Mould No.	Size	Quantity per Crate	Weight per Gross
J-51	4 oz.	3 gro.	50 lbs.

HEXAGON TOILET

Mould No.	Size	Quantity per Crate	Weight per Gross
J-76	4 oz.	3 gro.	50 lbs.

Perfume Bottles

TAPER PERFUME

Mould No.	Size	Quantity per Crate	Weight per Gross
T-187	½ oz.	5 gro.	15 lbs.
C-99	7 dr.	5 gro.	30 lbs.

TAPER OVAL PERFUME

Mould No.	Size	Quantity per Crate	Weight per Gross
J-59	1 oz.	5 gro.	20 lbs.

TALL TAPER PERFUMES

Mould No.	Size	Quantity per Crate	Weight per Gross
531	½ oz.	5 gro.	25 lbs.
K-98	7 dr.	3 gro.	35 lbs.

FLUTED PERFUME

Mould No.	Size	Quantity per Crate	Weight per Gross
F-76	6 dr.	5 gro.	30 lbs.

TAPER PERFUME

Mould No.	Size	Quantity per Crate	Weight per Gross
D-21	3½ dr.	5 gro.	25 lbs.

FLUTED PERFUME

Mould No.	Size	Quantity per Crate	Weight per Gross
963	½ oz.	5 gro.	25 lbs.

TAPER PERFUME

Mould No.	Size	Quantity per Crate	Weight per Gross
H-19	1 oz.	5 gro.	20 lbs.

TAPER RIBBED PERFUME

Mould No.	Size	Quantity per Crate	Weight per Gross
M-23	½ oz.	7 gro.	18 lbs.

Illinois Glass Company

Perfume Bottles

OBLONG PERFUME

Mould No.	Size	Quantity per Crate	Weight per Gross
L-11	1½ oz.	3 gro.	35 lbs.

FLAT OBLONG PERFUME

Mould No.	Size	Quantity per Crate	Weight per Gross
T-273	3 oz.	3 gro.	45 lbs.

OBLONG PERFUMES

Mould No.	Size	Quantity per Crate	Weight per Gross
G-55	½ oz.	5 gro.	15 lbs.
A-57	¾ oz.	5 gro.	20 lbs.

FLAT PERFUME

Mould No.	Size	Quantity per Crate	Weight per Gross
T-323	½ oz.	5 gro.	15 lbs.
Y-15	2 oz.	3 gro.	35 lbs.

FLAT OVAL PERFUME

Mould No.	Size	Quantity per Crate	Weight per Gross
2090	1 oz.	3 gro.	30 lbs.

KEYSTONE PERFUME

Mould No.	Size	Quantity per Crate	Weight per Gross
2254	½ oz.	10 gro.	15 lbs.
A-10	1 oz.	5 gro.	20 lbs.

SQUAT OBLONG PERFUME

Mould No.	Size	Quantity per Crate	Weight per Gross
K-76	6 dr.	3 gro.	30 lbs.

SQUAT TAPER PERFUME

Mould No.	Size	Quantity per Crate	Weight per Gross
L-4	6 dr.	3 gro.	35 lbs.

Perfume Bottles

OVAL PERFUMES

Mould No.	Size	Quantity per Crate	Weight per Gross
D-28	½ oz.	5 gro.	25 lbs.
J-35	1 oz.	5 gro.	30 lbs.

SCREW TOP TAPER PERFUMES

Mould No.	Size	Quantity per Crate	Weight per Gross
A-2	3½ dr.	6 gro.	20 lbs.
919	7 dr.	5 gro.	25 lbs.
F-73	1¼ oz.	3 gro.	35 lbs.

OVAL PANELED PERFUME

Mould No.	Size	Quantity per Crate	Weight per Gross
D-3	½ oz.	5 gro.	25 lbs.

TAPER HEXAGON PERFUME

Mould No.	Size	Quantity per Crate	Weight per Gross
454	½ oz.	5 gro.	25 lbs.

KEYSTONE PERFUME

Mould No.	Size	Quantity per Crate	Weight per Gross
H-53	½ oz.	10 gro.	15 lbs.

SQUARE PANEL PERFUME

Mould No.	Size	Quantity per Crate	Weight per Gross
H-97	1 oz.	5 gro.	30 lbs.

ROUND PERFUMES

Mould No.	Size	Quantity per Crate	Weight per Gross
D-27	½ oz.	5 gro.	25 lbs.
C-67	1 oz.	5 gro.	30 lbs.
D-90	2 oz.	3 gro.	40 lbs.

ROUND LUBIN

Mould No.	Size	Quantity per Crate	Weight per Gross
T-161	½ oz.	5 gro.	15 lbs.
J-48	1 oz.	5 gro.	25 lbs.

Perfume Bottles

TAPER SQUARE PERFUME

Mould No.	Size	Quantity per Crate	Weight per Gross
H-62	7 dr.	5 gro.	25 lbs.

SQUARE LUBINS

Mould No.	Size	Quantity per Crate	Weight per Gross
T-184	2 dr.	5 gro.	18 lbs.
T-40	3½ dr.	5 gro.	20 lbs.
K-45	½ oz.	5 gro.	20 lbs.

RECESSED COLOGNES

Mould No.	Size	Quantity per Crate	Weight per Gross
791	2 dr.	10 gro.	10 lbs
519	½ oz.	5 gro.	18 lbs.

PURSE PERFUMES

Mould No.	Size	Quantity per Crate	Weight per Gross
T-346	1½ dr.	10 gro.	6 lbs.

JUSTRITE PERFUME

Mould No.	Size	Quantity per Crate	Weight per Gross
T-207	⅛ oz.	10 gro.	6 lbs.

TALL SQUARE PERFUME

Mould No.	Size	Quantity per Crate	Weight per Gross
T-276	2 dr.	10 gro.	10 lbs.
Q-74	4 dr.	5 gro.	18 lbs.

OBLONG PERFUME

Mould No.	Size	Quantity per Crate	Weight per Gross
M-94	2 dr.	10 gro.	10 lbs.

MINIATURE CHAMPAGNE PERFUME

Mould No.	Size	Quantity per Crate	Weight per Gross
T-310	1 dr.	10 gro.	6 lbs.

Illinois Glass Company

Brilliantines, Sachet, Bandolines and Atomizers

ROUND BRILLIANTINE

Mould No.	Size	Quantity per Crate	Weight per Gross
2073	2 oz.	3 gro.	35 lbs.

SQUARE BRILLIANTINE

Mould No.	Size	Quantity per Crate	Weight per Gross
T-289	1 oz.	5 gro.	30 lbs.

TAPER FOOTED SACHET

Mould No.	Size	Quantity per Crate	Weight per Gross
M-52	1 oz.	5 gro.	25 lbs.

BANDOLINE

Mould No.	Size	Quantity per Crate	Weight per Gross
T-351	2 oz.	3 gro.	40 lbs.

BANDOLINE

Mould No.	Size	Quantity per Crate	Weight per Gross
G-53	2 oz.	3 gro.	35 lbs.

ATOMIZER BOTTLE

Mould No.	Size	Quantity per Crate	Weight per Gross
D-9	¾ oz.	5 gro.	18 lbs.

ATOMIZER BOTTLE

Mould No.	Size	Quantity per Crate	Weight per Gross
D-42	2⅜ oz.	3 gro.	35 lbs.

ATOMIZER BOTTLE

Mould No.	Size	Quantity per Crate	Weight per Gross
D-40	2½ oz.	3 gro.	35 lbs.

Illinois Glass Company

Toilet Cream Jars

THE plain, straight sided Toilet Cream Jar, illustrated above, is our leading package in this field. This jar is produced in clear flint glass, labels well and makes an attractive container.

Because of its wide mouth, it is satisfactory for either home or professional use.

Furnished complete with aluminum caps, if desired.

TOILET CREAM JARS

Mould No.	Size	Quantity per Crate	Weight per Gross
W-19-X	4 oz.	2 gro.	58 lbs.
N-57-X	8 oz.	1½ gro.	95 lbs.
N-58-X	16 oz.	1 gro.	140 lbs.

Toilet Cream Jars

TOILET CREAM JAR

Mould No.	Size	Quantity per Crate	Weight per Gross
C-44	6 oz.	1½ gro.	90 lbs.

ROUND TOILET CREAM JAR

Mould No.	Size	Quantity per Crate	Weight per Gross
Q-26	7 oz.	1½ gro.	90 lbs.

ROUND TOILET CREAM JAR

Mould No.	Size	Quantity per Crate	Weight per Gross
M-36	1½ oz.	5 gro.	25 lbs
M-37	3¾ oz.	3 gro.	45 lbs.

ROUND TOILET CREAM JAR

Mould No.	Size	Quantity per Crate	Weight per Gross
M-91	5 oz.	2 gro.	65 lbs.

ROUND FOOTED TOILET CREAM JAR

Mould No.	Size	Quantity per Crate	Weight per Gross
M-79	5 oz.	2 gro.	60 lbs.

Toilet Cream Jars

TAPER OBLONG TOILET CREAM JAR

Mould No.	Size	Quantity per Crate	Weight per Gross
P-38	2¾ oz.	3 gro.	45 lbs.

TAPER CONCAVE TOILET CREAM JAR

Mould No.	Size	Quantity per Crate	Weight per Gross
M-88	3 oz.	3 gro.	60 lbs.

TAPER SQUARE TOILET CREAM JAR

Mould No.	Size	Quantity per Crate	Weight per Gross
614	3 oz.	2 gro.	55 lbs.

TAPER OBLONG TOILET CREAM JARS

Mould No.	Size	Quantity per Crate	Weight per Gross
T-198	1½ oz.	3 gro.	45 lbs.

SQUARE TOILET CREAM JAR

Mould No.	Size	Quantity per Crate	Weight per Gross
L-43	3 oz.	3 gro.	60 lbs.

CONCAVE TOILET CREAM JARS

Mould No.	Size	Quantity per Crate	Weight per Gross
G-72	2 oz.	2 gro.	60 lbs.
G-73	5 oz.	1½ gro.	80 lbs.

Pomades, Toilet Creams, and Bath Salts

ROUND POMADES

Mould No.	Size	Quantity per Crate	Weight per Gross
L-37	1¼ oz.	3 gro.	22 lbs.
R-14	1½ oz.	5 gro.	35 lbs.
Q-14	1⅝ oz.	5 gro.	35 lbs.
N-21-X	2 oz.	4 gro.	35 lbs.
N-76-X	4 oz.	3 gro.	50 lbs.
N-77-X	5 oz.	2 gro.	60 lbs.

ROUND TAPER TOILET CREAM JAR

Mould No.	Size	Quantity per Crate	Weight per Gross
T-317	2 oz.	3 gro.	35 lbs.

ROUND POMADE CORK FINISH

Mould No.	Size	Quantity per Crate	Weight per Gross
G-18	2 oz.	5 gro.	30 lbs.
J-28	3 oz.	3 gro.	40 lbs.

SQUARE BATH SALTS

Mould No.	Size	Quantity per Crate	Weight per Gross
B-7	8 oz.	1 gro.	90 lbs.

OBLONG RIBBED BATH SALTS

Mould No.	Size	Quantity per Crate	Weight per Gross
2086	6 oz.	2 gro.	70 lbs.

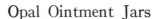

Opal Ointment Jars

THE Package Sizes and Weight per gross are approximate.

These styles have a beaded top and bottom.

Unless otherwise specified, the jars are packed in 1 and 2 dozen Cardboard Boxes, complete with Aluminum or Nickel Plated Caps.

Lettered jars or lettered caps cannot be supplied.

TALL OPAL OINTMENTS

Mould No.	Size	Quantity per Crate	Weight per Gross
19	¼ oz.	10 gro.	13 lbs.
20	½ oz.	5 gro.	20 lbs.
21	1 oz.	3 gro.	35 lbs.
22	2 oz.	2 gro.	60 lbs.
23	3 oz.	2 gro.	73 lbs.
24	4 oz.	2 gro.	100 lbs.

THE Package Sizes and Weight per gross are approximate.

These styles have straight sides and no beads.

Unless otherwise specified, the jars, except the 8 and 16-ounce sizes, are packed in 1 and 2 dozen Cardboard Boxes, complete with Aluminum or Nickel Plated Caps. The 8 and 16-ounce jars are supplied in bulk only.

Lettered jars or lettered caps cannot be supplied.

SQUAT OPAL OINTMENTS

Mould No.	Size	Quantity per Crate	Weight per Gross
40	¼ oz.	10 gro.	14 lbs.
41	½ oz.	5 gro.	23 lbs.
42	1 oz.	3 gro.	52 lbs.
43	2 oz.	3 gro.	57 lbs.
44	3 oz.	2 gro.	90 lbs.
45	4 oz.	2 gro.	95 lbs.
46	8 oz.	1 gro.	168 lbs.
47	16 oz.	½ gro.	280 lbs.

Opal Ointment Jars

THE Package Sizes and Weight per gross are approximate.

These styles have a beaded top and bottom, and can be furnished with either ribbed or plain sides.

Unless otherwise specified, the jars are packed in 1 and 2 dozen Cardboard Boxes, complete with Aluminum or Nickel Plated Caps.

Lettered jars or lettered caps cannot be supplied.

SQUARE OPAL OINTMENTS

Mould No.	Size	Quantity per Case	Weight per Gross
1996	¼ oz.	5 gro.	22 lbs.
1968	½ oz.	5 gro.	31 lbs.
1256	1 oz.	3 gro.	57 lbs.
1208	2 oz.	2 gro.	90 lbs.
1257	4 oz.	2 gro.	120 lbs.

INDENTED OPAL PATCH BOXES

Mould No.	Size	Quantity per Bbl.	Weight per Gross
00	⅛ oz.	25 gro.	13 lbs.
0	¼ oz.	12 gro.	21 lbs.
1	½ oz.	8 gro.	33 lbs.
2	1 oz.	5¼ gro.	50 lbs.
10	1½ oz.	5¼ gro.	44 lbs.
3	2 oz.	2½ gro.	90 lbs.

FLAT OPAL PATCH BOXES

Mould No.	Size	Quantity per Bbl.	Weight per Gross
00	⅛ oz.	25 gro.	13 lbs.
0	¼ oz.	12 gro.	21 lbs.
6	½ oz.	8 gro.	33 lbs.
7	1 oz.	5¼ gro.	47 lbs.
10½	1½ oz.	4½ gro.	50 lbs.
8	2 oz.	2½ gro.	82 lbs.

Perfumes

MOULD C H No. 232

Size		Weight per Gross
½ oz.	C H No. 441 GGS	32 lbs.
1 oz.	C H No. 442 GGS	45 lbs.
3½ oz.	C H No. 443 GGS	77 lbs.

MOULD C H No. 232

Size		Weight per Gross
½ oz.	C H No. 397 GGS	32 lbs.
1 oz.	C H No. 398 GGS	45 lbs.
3½ oz.	C H No. 403 GGS	77 lbs.

MOULD C H No. 237

Size		Weight per Gross
1 oz.	C H No. 428 GGS	38 lbs.

MOULD C H No. 234

Size		Weight per Gross
7 dr.	C H No. 391 GGS	40 lbs.

MOULD C H No. 229

Size		Weight per Gross
½ oz.	C H No. 395 GGS	35 lbs.
1 oz.	C H No. 395 GGS	45 lbs.
3½ oz.	C H No. 402 GGS	77 lbs.

Perfumes

MOULD C H No. 121

Size		Weight per Gross
6 dr.	C H No. 222 GGS	34 lbs.

MOULD C H No. 177

Size		Weight per Gross
1 oz.	C H No. 360 GGS	45 lbs.
3½ oz.	C H No. 346 GGS	75 lbs.

For Machine Made Perfume and Toilet Ware see Pages 72 to 98 inclusive.

MOULD C H No. 139

Size		Weight per Gross
½ oz.	C H No. 216 GGS	18 lbs.

MOULD C H No. 177

Size		Weight per Gross
1 oz.	C H No. 308 GGS	45 lbs.

MOULD C H No. 243

Size		Weight per Gross
1 oz.	C H No. 443 GGS	46 lbs.

MOULD C H No. 65

Size		Weight per Gross
1 oz.	C H No. 308 GGS	35 lbs.

MOULD C H No. 68

Size		Weight per Gross
7 dr.	C H No. 255 GGS	33 lbs.

MOULD C H No. 122

Size		Weight per Gross
4 oz.	C H No. 294 GGS	80 lbs.

Perfumes

MOULD C H No. 90

Size	Weight per Gross
½ oz.	24 lbs.

MOULD C H No. 88

Size	Weight per Gross
2 dr.	14½ lbs.

MOULD C H No. 27

Size		Weight per Gross
½ oz.	C H No. 261 GGS	21 lbs.
1 oz.	C H No. 261 GGS	30 lbs.
2 oz.		30 lbs.
2¼ oz.		51 lbs.
3½ oz.	C H No. 255 GGS	72 lbs.
4 oz.		90 lbs.
5½ oz.		84 lbs.

MOULD C H No. 87

Size	Weight per Gross
½ oz.	15 lbs.

MOULD C H No. 287

Size		Weight per Gross
3 dr.	C H No. 216 GGS	15 lbs.
7 dr.	C H No. 222 GGS	34 lbs.

MOULD C H No. 41

Size	Weight per Gross
½ oz.	24 lbs.
1 oz.	31 lbs.
8 oz.	120 lbs.

MOULD C H No. 10

Size	Weight per Gross
½ oz.	24 lbs.
1 oz.	33 lbs.
1½ oz.	42 lbs.
3 oz.	66 lbs.

MOULD C H No. 23

Size	Weight per Gross
1 oz.	36 lbs.
2 oz.	48 lbs.

Illinois Glass Company

Perfumes

MOULD C H No. 80

Size	Weight per Gross
1½ oz.	36 lbs.

MOULD C H No. 167

Size	Weight per Gross
1 oz.	36 lbs.

MOULD C H No. 82

Size	Weight per Gross
¾ oz.	33 lbs.
Furnished also with C H No. 328 GGS	43 lbs.

MOULD C H No. 4

Size	Weight per Gross
¾ oz.	18 lbs.
Furnished also with C H No. 227 GGS	27 lbs.

MOULD C H No. 5

Size	Weight per Gross
1 oz.	31 lbs.
Furnished also with C H No. 294 GGS	40 lbs.

MOULD C H No. 116

Size	Weight per Gross
½ oz.	18 lbs.

MOULD C H No. 233

Size	Weight per Gross
2 oz.	46 lbs.

MOULD C H No. 175

Size	Weight per Gross
1 dr.	3 lbs.

MOULD C H No. 212

Size	Weight per Gross
2 oz.	48 lbs.

Illinois Glass Company

Perfumes

MOULD C H No. 126—RD. LUBIN

Size		Weight per Gross
½ oz.	C H No. 227 GGS	22 lbs.
1 oz.	C H No. 376 GGS	34 lbs.
2 oz.	C H No. 376 GGS	49 lbs.
4 oz.	C H No. 377 GGS	64 lbs.

MOULD C H No. 127 SQUARE LUBIN

Size		Weight per Gross
½ oz.	C H No. 227 GGS	28 lbs.
¾ oz.	C H No. 227 GGS	30 lbs.
1 oz.	C H No. 376 GGS	34 lbs.
2 oz.	C H No. 376 GGS	49 lbs.
2½ oz.	C H No. 377 GGS	45 lbs.

MOULD C H No. 126

Size		Weight per Gross
½ oz.	C H No. 424 GGS	23 lbs.
1 oz.	C H No. 366 GGS	35 lbs.
2 oz.	C H No. 366 GGS	50 lbs.
4 oz.	C H No. 238 GGS	65 lbs.

MOULD C H No. 84

Size	Weight per Gross
½ oz.	26 lbs.

MOULD C H No. 67

Size		Weight per Gross
1 oz.	C H No. 238 GGS	34 lbs.
1¼ oz.	C H No. 238 GGS	34 lbs.

MOULD C H No. 194

Size		Weight per Gross
1 oz.	C H No. 357 GGS	49 lbs.

MOULD C H No. 112

Size	Weight per Gross
½ oz.	21 lbs.
Furnished also with C H No. 255 GGS	30 lbs.

MOULD C H No. 110

Size	Weight per Gross
½ oz.	21 lbs.
Furnished also with C H No. 255 GGS	30 lbs.

Perfumes

MOULD C H No. 284

Size	Weight per Gross
2 oz.	30 lbs.

MOULD C H No. 133

Size	Weight per Gross
¼ oz.	6 lbs.
½ oz.	18 lbs.
2 oz.	27 lbs.

MOULD C H No. 146

Size	Weight per Gross
2 oz.	32 lbs.

MOULD C H No. 70

Size	Weight per Gross
7 dr.	36 lbs.

MOULD C H No. 190

Size	Weight per Gross
7 dr.	35 lbs.
3½ oz.	72 lbs.
The 7 dram size is also furnished with C H No. 343 GGS	40 lbs.

MOULD C H No. 238

Size	Weight per Gross
3 dr.	13 lbs.

MOULD C H No. 200

Size		Weight per Gross
6 dr.	C H No. 220 GGS	34 lbs.

MOULD C H No. 105

Size		Weight per Gross
½ oz.	C H No. 308 GGS	25 lbs.
1 oz.	C H No. 308 GGS	38 lbs.

Perfumes

MOULD C H No. 202

Size	Weight per Gross
2 dr. CH No. 356 *EGGS	10 lbs.

MOULD C H No. 58

Size	Weight per Gross
1 dr. CH No. 355 *EGGS	9 lbs.
1½ dr. CH No. 355 *EGGS	9 lbs.

MOULD C H No. 196

Size		Weight per Gross
¼ oz.	C H No. 355 *EGGS	9 lbs.

MOULD C H No. 166

Size		Weight per Gross
1 oz.	C H No. 327 GGS	30 lbs.

MOULD C H No. 245

Size	Weight per Gross
½ oz. C H No. 424 GGS	29 lbs.

MOULD C H No. 91

Size	½ oz.	1 oz.	2 oz.	3 oz.
Stopper CH No.	201	202	203	203
Wt. per gross	41	42	55	60 lbs.
Size	4 oz.	8 oz.	16 oz.	
Stopper CH No.	204	205	206	
Wt. per gross	69	150	212 lbs.	

MOULD C H No. 69

Size		Weight per Gross
6 dr.	C H No. 253 GGS	37 lbs.
1 oz.	C H No. 253 GGS	43 lbs.
2 oz.	C H No. 253 GGS	45 lbs.

MOULD C H No. 30

Size	Weight per Gross
½ oz. C H No. 293 GGS	35 lbs.
1 oz. C H No. 294 GGS	50 lbs.
1 oz. C H No. 357 GGS	50 lbs.

MOULD C H No. 6

Size		Weight per Gross
1 oz.	C H No. 255 GGS	36 lbs.

Note: EGGS denotes Elongated Ground Glass Stopper.

Perfumes

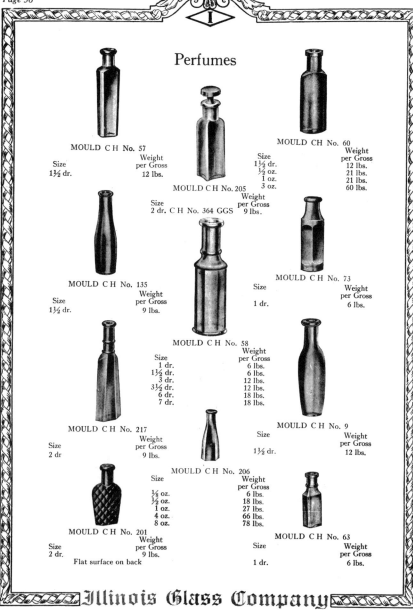

MOULD C H No. 57

Size	Weight per Gross
1½ dr.	12 lbs.

MOULD C H No. 205

Size	Weight per Gross
2 dr. C H No. 364 GGS	9 lbs.

MOULD C H No. 60

Size	Weight per Gross
1½ dr.	12 lbs.
½ oz.	21 lbs.
1 oz.	21 lbs.
3 oz.	60 lbs.

MOULD C H No. 135

Size	Weight per Gross
1½ dr.	9 lbs.

MOULD C H No. 73

Size	Weight per Gross
1 dr.	6 lbs.

MOULD C H No. 58

Size	Weight per Gross
1 dr.	6 lbs.
1½ dr.	6 lbs.
3 dr.	12 lbs.
3½ dr.	12 lbs.
6 dr.	18 lbs.
7 dr.	18 lbs.

MOULD C H No. 217

Size	Weight per Gross
2 dr	9 lbs.

MOULD C H No. 9

Size	Weight per Gross
1½ dr.	12 lbs.

MOULD C H No. 206

Size	Weight per Gross
⅛ oz.	6 lbs.
½ oz.	18 lbs.
1 oz.	27 lbs.
4 oz.	66 lbs.
8 oz.	78 lbs.

MOULD C H No. 201

Size	Weight per Gross
2 dr.	9 lbs.

Flat surface on back

MOULD C H No. 63

Size	Weight per Gross
1 dr.	6 lbs.

Perfumes and Toilet Waters

MOULD C H No. 189

Size		Weight per Gross
½ oz.	C H No. 349 GGS	26 lbs.
1 oz.	C H No. 349 GGS	40 lbs.
3 oz.	Cork Finish	72 lbs.

MOULD C H No. 192

Size		Weight per Gross
3½ oz.	C H No. 354 GGS	90 lbs.

MOULD C H No. 293

Size		Weight per Gross
1 oz.	C H No. 216 GGS	45 lbs.
4 oz.	Cork Finish	72 lbs.

MOULD C H No. 190

Size		Weight per Gross
7 dr.	Peg Stopper and Shell Cork	35 lbs.
3½ oz.	Peg Stopper and Shell Cork	78 lbs.

MOULD C H No. 180

Size		Weight per Gross
3½ oz.	C H No. 221 GGS	110 lbs.

MOULD C H No. 179

Size		Weight per Gross
½ oz.	C H No. 216 GGS	20 lbs.
1 oz.	C H No. 308 GGS	33 lbs.
4 oz.	C H No. 350 GGS	80 lbs.

Illinois Glass Company

Perfumes and Toilet Waters

MOULD C H No. 78

Size		Weight Per Gross
1 oz.	C H No. 315 GGS	39 lbs.
4 oz.	C H No. 303	
	Peg Stopper	78 lbs.

MOULD C H No. 108

Size	Weight per Gross
4 oz.	66 lbs.

MOULD C H No. 40

Size	Weight per Gross
3½ oz.	66 lbs.
4 oz.	72 lbs.
5 oz.	96 lbs.

MOULD C H No. 219

Size		Weight per Gross
1 oz.	Cork Finish	33 lbs.
4 oz.	Cork Finish	72 lbs.

MOULD C H No. 13

Size	Weight per Gross
4 oz.	60 lbs.
Furnished also with C H No. 255 GGS	85 lbs.

MOULD C H No. 244

Size	Weight per Gross
4½ oz.	65 lbs.

Perfumes and Toilet Water

MOULD C H No. 35

Size	Weight per Gross
3 oz.	54 lbs.
4 oz.	66 lbs.
8 oz.	76 lbs.

MOULD C H No. 106

Size	Weight per Gross
6 oz.	72 lbs.

MOULD C H No. 25

Size	Weight per Gross
2 oz.	48 lbs.
4 oz.	60 lbs.

MOULD C H No. 99

Size	Weight per Gross
2½ oz.	54 lbs.
6 oz.	72 lbs.

MOULD C H No. 32

Size	¾ oz.	1 oz.	1½ oz.	2 oz.
Wt. per gro.	18 lbs.	24 lbs.	30 lbs.	36 lbs.
Size	3 oz.	4 oz.	7½ oz.	16 oz.
Wt. per gro.	42 lbs.	60 lbs.	84 lbs.	144 lbs.

MOULD C H No. 39

Size	½ oz.	1 oz.	2 oz.	3 oz.
Wt. per gro.	14 lbs.	21 lbs.	30 lbs.	48 lbs.
Size	4 oz.	6 oz.	8 oz.	
Wt. per gro.	66 lbs.	72 lbs.	100 lbs.	

Perfumes and Toilet Water

MOULD C H No. 199

Size	Weight per Gross
4 oz.	66 lbs.
4 oz. C H No. 290 GGS	90 lbs.

Note—C H No. 251 4 oz. Toilet Water is the same as the bottle illustrated except that it is plain.

MOULD C H No. 49

Size	2 oz.	3½ oz.	4 oz.	6 oz.
Wt. per gro.	30 lbs.	42 lbs.	66 lbs.	72 lbs.

Size	8 oz.	10 oz.	12 oz.
Wt. per gro.	90 lbs.	108 lbs.	132 lbs.

MOULD C H No. 221

Size	Weight per Gross
2 oz.	36 lbs.
3 lbs.	50 lbs.
5½ oz.	72 lbs.

For Machine Made Perfume and Toilet Ware see Pages 72 to 98 inclusive.

MOULD C H No. 230

Size	Weight per Gross
2 oz.	40 lbs.
3 oz.	48 lbs.
4 lbs.	66 lbs.

MOULD C H No. 50

Size	Weight per Gross
6 oz.	96 lbs.

Can Be Lettered

MOULD C H No. 66

Size	2 oz.	3 oz.	4 oz.	6 oz.
Wt. per gro.	24 lbs.	33 lbs.	48 lbs.	66 lbs.

Size	8 oz.	12 oz.	16 oz.
Wt. per gro.	84 lbs.	99 lbs.	144 lbs.

Perfumes and Toilet Water

MOULD C H No. 227

Size   Weight per Gross

16 oz.   Cork Finish   140 lbs.

MOULD C H No. 292

Size   Weight per Gross

7 oz.   96 lbs.

MOULD C H No. 311

Size   Weight per Gross

12 oz.   129 lbs.

16 oz.   144 lbs.

MOULD C H No. 3

Size	2 oz.	3 oz.	4 oz.	6 oz.
Wt. per gro.	27 lbs.	36 lbs.	54 lbs.	66 lbs.
Size	8 oz.	12 oz.	16 oz.	32 oz.
Wt. per gro.	84 lbs.	120 lbs.	144 lbs.	240 lbs.

MOULD C H No. 134

Size   Weight per Gross

10 oz.   90 lbs.

With Oval Plate for Lettering

Perfumes, Toilet Waters and Toilet Creams

TOILET CREAM
MOULD C H No. 47

Size	Weight per Gross
1½ oz.	24 lbs.
2 oz.	30 lbs.
3 oz.	42 lbs.
4 oz.	54 lbs.

GOTHIC TOILET
MOULD C H No. 55

Size	Weight per Gross
2 oz.	36 lbs.
3 oz.	48 lbs.
4 oz.	72 lbs.
6 oz.	96 lbs.

Can also be supplied paneled on
edges only

MOULD C H No. 193

Size	Weight per Gross
3 oz.	58 lbs.

Furnished also with
C H No. 389 GGS 65 lbs.

*For Machine Made Perfume and
Toilet Ware see Pages 72 to 98 inclusive.*

For Machine Made Perfume and Toilet Ware see Pages 72 to 98 inclusive.

MOULD C H No. 300

Size	½ oz.	1 oz.	2 oz.	3 oz.	4 oz.
Wt. per gro.	12 lb.	15 lb.	30 lb.	39 lb.	54 lb.

Size	6 oz.	8 oz.	12 oz.	16 oz.	32 oz.
Wt. per gro.	70 lb.	84 lb.	132 lb.	168 lb.	240 lb.

MOULD C H No. 301

Size	1 oz.	2 oz.	3 oz.	4 oz.
Wt. per gro.	21 lbs.	30 lbs.	42 lbs.	48 lbs.

Size	8 oz.	12 oz.	16 oz.
Wt. per gro.	84 lbs.	120 lbs.	144 lbs.

Bulk Perfumes

MOULD C H No. 2

Size		Weight per Gross
½ oz.	C H No. 304 GGS	29 lbs.
1 oz.	C H No. 305 GGS	40 lbs.
8 oz.	C H No. 249 GGS	136 lbs.

MOULD C H No. 187

Size		Weight per Gross
8¼ oz.	C H No. 307 GGS	145 lbs.

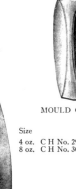

MOULD C H No. 79

Size		Weight per Gross
4 oz.	C H No. 295 GGS	72 lbs.
8 oz.	C H No. 307 GGS	144 lbs.

MOULD C H No. 279

Size		Weight per Gross
4 oz.	Cork Finish	60 lbs.
8 oz.	C H No. 290 GGS	114 lbs.

MOULD C H No. 92

Size		Weight per Gross
8 oz.	C H No. 302 GGS	140 lbs.

Bulk Perfumes

MOULD C H No. 159

Size		Weight per Gross
18 oz.	C H No. 215 GGS	147 lbs.

MOULD C H No. 247

Size		Weight per Gross
8 oz.	C H No. 249 GGS	132 lbs.

MOULD C H No. 149

Size		Weight per Gross
8 oz.	C H No. 257 GGS	150 lbs.

MOULD C H No. 131

Size		Weight per Gross
8 oz.	C H No. 257 GGS	136 lbs.

Also furnished with C H No. 254 Peg
stopper—Shell Cork

MOULD C H No. 188

Size		Weight per Gross
8¼ oz.	C H No. 249 GGS	145 lbs.

Illinois Glass Company

Bulk Perfumes

MOULD C H No. 17

Size		Weight per Gross
4 oz.	C H No. 214 GGS	70 lbs.
8 oz.	C H No. 215 GGS	140 lbs.
16 oz.	C H No. 215 GGS	165 lbs.

MOULD C H No. 93

Size		Weight per Gross
8 oz.	C H No. 307 GGS	140 lbs.

MOULD C H No. 162

Size		Weight per Gross
8 oz.	C H No. 323 GGS	132 lbs.

MOULD C H No. 151

Size		Weight per Gross
8 oz.	C H No. 307 GGS	115 lbs.

MOULD C H No. 18

Size		Weight per Gross
4 oz.	C H No. 214 GGS	75 lbs.
8 oz.	C H No. 215 GGS	130 lbs.
16 oz.	C H No. 215 GGS	150 lbs.

MOULD C H No. 20

Size		Weight per Gross
8 oz.	C H No. 215 GGS	128 lbs.
16 oz.	C H No. 215 GGS	160 lbs.

Barber Stand Bottles

MOULD C H No. 195

Size   Weight per Gross
10 oz.   155 lbs.

MOULD C H No. 249

Size   Weight per Gross
10 oz.   110 lbs.

MOULD C H No. 252

Size   Weight per Gross
21⅛ oz.   260 lbs.

MOULD C H No. 222

Size   Weight per Gross
7 oz.   96 lbs.

MOULD C H No. 231

Size   Weight per Gross
10 oz.   120 lbs.

MOULD C H No. 155

Size   Weight per Gross
7 oz.   96 lbs.

Illinois Glass Company

Sachet Powders

MOULD C H No. 140

Size	Weight per Gross
5 dr. Brass Screw Cap	24 lbs.
1¼ oz. Brass Screw Cap	36 lbs.

MOULD C H No. 290

Size	Weight per Gross
½ oz.	12 lbs.
1 oz.	20 lbs.

MOULD C H No. 185

Size	Weight per Gross
1 oz. Brass Screw Cap	39 lbs.

MOULD C H No. 296

Size	Weight per Gross
1 oz.	30 lbs.

MOULD C H No. 154

Size	Weight per Gross
1 oz. Brass Screw Cap	42 lbs.

MOULD C H No. 281

Size	Weight per Gross
¼ oz. Brass Screw Cap	8 lbs.
½ oz. Brass Screw Cap	24 lbs.

MOULD C H No. 148

Size	Weight per Gross
2 oz.	36 lbs.

ROUGE OR NAIL POLISH
MOULD C H No. 282

Size	Weight per Gross
½ oz.	9 lbs.

Bandolines and Tooth Powders

MOULD C H No. 53

Size	Weight per Gross
2 oz.	60 lbs.
4 oz.	81 lbs.
4½ oz.	81 lbs.

TOOTH WASH
Mould C H No. 102

Size		Weight per Gross
2 oz.	Plain	48 lbs.
Mould C H No. 103—Paneled		48 lbs.

For Machine Made Perfume and Toilet Ware see Pages 72 to 98 inclusive.

MOULD C H No. 308

Size	Weight per Gross
2⅛ oz.	42 lbs.

MOULD C H No. 306

Size	Weight per Gross
½ oz.	21 lbs.
2 oz.	48 lbs.

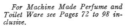

MOULD C H No. 309

Size	Weight per Gross
2 oz.	45 lbs.

MOULD C H No. 143

Size	Weight per Gross
2 oz.	30 lbs.

MOULD C H No. 184

Size	Weight per Gross
2 oz.	36 lbs.

MOULD C H No. 313

Size	Weight per Gross
2 oz.	36 lbs.

Cold Creams

MOULD C H No. 164

Size 3 oz. C H No. 256 GGS

Weight per Gross 48 lbs.

MOULD C H No. 104

Size 3 oz. C H No. 213 GGS

Weight per Gross 70 lbs.

MOULD C H No. 101

Size 3 oz. C H No. 256 GGS

Weight per Gross 70 lbs.

MOULD C H No. 111

Size 4 oz. C H No. 314 GGS

Weight per Gross 95 lbs.

MOULD C H No. 181

Size 2 oz.

Weight per Gross 52 lbs.

MOULD C H No. 21

Size 3 oz. C H No. 276-M GGS

Weight per Gross 70 lbs.

MOULD C H No. 100

Size 2½ oz. C H No. 256 GGS

Weight per Gross 62 lbs.

MOULD C H No. 100

Size 2½ oz. C H No. 300 GGS

Weight per Gross 62 lbs.

MOULD C H No. 211

Size 2¾ oz. C H No. 228 GGS

Weight per Gross 60 lbs.

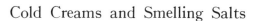

Cold Creams and Smelling Salts

MOULD C H No. 253

Size   Weight
           per Gross
1½ oz.   C H No. 272 GGS   45 lbs.

MOULD C H No. 225

Size   Weight
           per Gross
1 oz.   C H No. 272 GGS   50 lbs.

MOULD C H No. 1

Size   Weight
           per Gross
2 oz.   C H No. 212 GGS   64 lbs.

Bath Salts

MOULD C H No. 250

Size   Weight
           per Gross
8 oz.   100 lbs.

MOULD C H No. 261

Size	Weight per Gross
8 oz.	100 lbs.
12 oz.	130 lbs.
18 oz.	210 lbs.

MOULD C H No. 246

Size	Weight per Gross
8 oz.	100 lbs.
16 oz.	170 lbs.

Talcum Powders

MOULD C H No. 182

Size	Weight per Gross
5 oz.	78 lbs.

MOULD C H No. 226

Size	Weight per Gross
4 oz.	80 lbs.

MOULD C H No. 160

Size	Weight per Gross
4 oz.	65 lbs.

For Machine Made Perfume and Toilet Ware see Pages 72 to 98 inclusive.

MOULD C H No. 153

Size	Weight per Gross
4 oz.	78 lbs.

MOULD C H No. 94

Size	Weight per Gross
5 oz.	65 lbs.

MOULD C H No. 178

Size	Weight per Gross
4 oz.	65 lbs.

Talcum Powders

MOULD C H No. 85

Size	Weight per Gross
5 oz.	72 lbs.

MOULD C H No. 147

Size	Weight per Gross
5 oz.	72 lbs.

MOULD C H No. 125

Size	Weight per Gross
5¼ oz.	72 lbs.

MOULD C H No. 7

Size	Weight per Gross
4 oz.	72 lbs.

MOULD C H No. 254

Size	Weight per Gross
4¾ oz.	90 lbs.

MOULD C H No. 19

Size	Weight per Gross
3¾ oz.	54 lbs.

MOULD C H No. 11

Size	Weight per Gross
5 oz.	66 lbs.

MOULD C H No. 43

Size	Weight per Gross
5 oz.	66 lbs.

Shelf Ware

SHOP FURNITURE

STANDARD TINCTURE

Size	Height, with Stopper	Weight per Gross
1 oz.	3⅞ inches	18 lbs.
2 oz.	4¾ inches	27 lbs.
4 oz.	6 inches	54 lbs.
8 oz.	7 inches	84 lbs.
16 oz.	10¼ inches	144 lbs.
32 oz.	10⅜ inches	240 lbs.
½ gal.	12¾ inches	384 lbs.
1 gal.	14½ inches	600 lbs.
2 gal.	19½ inches	960 lbs.

COLUMBIAN TINCTURE
RECESSED

Size	Height, with Stopper	Weight per Gross
4 oz.	6¼ inches	66 lbs.
8 oz.	7¼ inches	95 lbs.
16 oz.	9⅜ inches	175 lbs.
32 oz.	10⅜ inches	320 lbs.
½ gal.	12⅜ inches	450 lbs.

CONGRESS TINCTURE
RECESSED

Size	Height, with Stopper	Weight per Gross
4 oz.	6 inches	66 lbs.
8 oz.	8¾ inches	95 lbs.
16 oz.	6⅜ inches	175 lbs.
32 oz.	10¼ inches	320 lbs.
64 oz.	12⅜ inches	450 lbs.

Shelf Ware
SHOP FURNITURE

STANDARD SALT MOUTH

Size	Height with Stopper	Weight per Gross
1 oz.	3¼ inches	18 lbs.
2 oz.	4⅝ inches	27 lbs.
4 oz.	5⅝ inches	54 lbs.
8 oz.	7 inches	84 lbs.
16 oz.	8¾ inches	144 lbs.
32 oz.	10¼ inches	240 lbs.
½ gal.	12½ inches	384 lbs.
1 gal.	14½ inches	600 lbs.
2 oz.	18¼ inches	960 lbs.

COLUMBIAN SALT MOUTH
RECESSED

Size	Height with Stopper	Weight per Gross
4 oz.	5¾ inches	66 lbs.
8 oz.	7 inches	95 lbs.
16 oz.	9 inches	175 lbs.
32 oz.	10¾ inches	320 lbs.
½ gal.	12½ inches	450 lbs.

CONGRESS SALT MOUTH
RECESSED

Size	Height with Stopper	Weight per Gross
4 oz.	5⅝ inches	70 lbs.
8 oz.	6¾ inches	100 lbs.
16 oz.	8¼ inches	175 lbs.
32 oz.	10 inches	320 lbs.
64 oz.	12 inches	450 lbs.

Candy Jars

C H No. 3-5 lb.—C H No. 75 GG Stopper
Total Height, 12 inches
Height to Base of Neck, 8½ inches
Recessed Label Space, 3⅝ wide x 2⅞ inches high
Size, 5 x 5 inches square
Inside diameter of neck at shoulder, 3¹⁄₁₆ inches
Weight per gross 800 lbs. complete
Also Furnished with C H No. 384 Drop Stopper

C H No. 2-4 lb.—C H No. 75 GG Stopper
Total Height, 11½ inches
Height to Base of Neck, 8 inches
4¾ x 4¾ inches square
Inside neck diameter at shoulder, 3¹⁄₁₆ inches
Weight per gross 720 lbs. complete
Also Furnished with No. 384 Drop Stopper

Note: C H No. 2 is the same in appearance as C H No. 3, illustrated, except that it is unpaneled.

C H No. 3

C H No. 1-4 lb.—C H No. 75, GG Stopper
Total Height, 11 inches
Height to Base of Neck, 7⅞ inches
4⅞ x 4⅞ inches square
Inside neck diameter at shoulder, 3¹⁄₁₆ inches
Weight per gross 720 lbs. complete
Also Furnished with C H No. 384 Drop Stopper

C H No. 1-4½ lb.—C H No. 359 GG Stopper
New Style Garwood
Total Height, 11½ inches
Height to Base of Neck, 8 inches
5 x 5 inches square
Inside neck diameter at shoulder, 3½ inches
Weight per gross 720 lbs. complete
Also Furnished with No. 384 Drop Stopper

C H No. 1-5 lb.—C H No. 75 GG Stopper
Total Height, 13 inches
Height to Base of Neck, 9½ inches
4¾ x 4¾ inches square
Inside neck diameter at shoulder, 3¹⁄₁₆ inches
Weight per gross 720 lbs. complete
Also Furnished with No. 384 Drop Stopper

C H No. 1

Miscellaneous Equipment Made of Glass

Fire Extinguisher

THE Fire Extinguishers on this page are typical of some of the glass specialties we blow by hand at our Factory in Chicago Heights, Ill.

One of the advantages of the hand blown operation, of course, is the fact that it doesn't take the elaborate and expensive mould equipment required by the Automatic Machine.

Small orders and special shapes can thus be made by hand that would be prohibitive in cost if manufactured on the machine.

Although the Illinois Glass Company is one of the largest operators of Automatic Bottle Blowing Mechanisms in the world, it has maintained a hand blown plant of its own for many years in recognition of the legitimate place of this ancient process in giving a complete bottle service.

We are thus permitted to take care of small orders as well as of large.

THERE is no excuse, of course, for an empty fire extinguisher, especially if it is made of glass and the liquid is always visible. These containers are not offered as stock items but indicate the general type of this ware we are prepared to produce.

Fire Extinguisher

Glass Parts of Equipment

Vending Globe

Vending Globe

VENDING Globes for dispensing peanuts, candy coated chewing gum balls, etc. constitute another product of our hand blown facilities. These globes are not offered as stock items but illustrate what we can make if you are interested in containers for vending purposes.

Oiler

Oiler

ALL-GLASS Oilers, like those shown above, indicate how some concerns are getting away from the combination oil cups made with metal tops and bottoms and glass cylinder walls. These Oilers are not offered as stock items but indicate what we are prepared to produce along this line.

Glass Parts of Equipment

Soap Vender

GLASS Soap Globes are a modern institution fully in keeping with the present day emphasis on public hygiene and sanitation. While the containers illustrated on this page are private mould designs they indicate the type of ware we are prepared to produce for vending liquid soaps.

Soap Vender

Soap Vender

Illinois Glass Company

Plain Sample Oils

OIL displayed in our Sample Oil Bottles is well displayed.

These bottles are seamless, crystal clear, sparkling, and water white in color.

Preliminary viscosity and color tests are easily made, when your samples are submitted in these containers, and the advantage of a good "first impression" is gained.

Our Sample Oil Bottles are furnished in the popular 2 oz., 4 oz., and 8 oz. sizes, with ground and polished bottoms, if desired.

Plain Sample Oil

Lettered Sample Oils

A LETTERED Sample Oil Bottle, such as that illustrated at the right, has the very desirable feature of never losing its identity.

When your trade mark or name is blown in the glass, it is there to stay. It can't come off like a paper label and make an orphan of your sample.

While there is a slight charge to cover the making of the lettered moulds, it is really insignificent compared to the advantage of having your samples positively identified at all times and in all places.

Lettered Sample Oils, the same as plain stock bottles, are available with ground and polished bottoms if desired.

Lettered Sample Oil

PEG STOPPERS

THE assortment of distinctive Peg Stoppers illustrated on the following pages are actual size and can be supplied frosted or plain with shell corks, cut to fit, if desired.

We also manufacture a variety of Ground Glass Stoppers at our Chicago Heights Factory and are in position to produce Stoppers of special private mould design, if preferred.

Permit us to assist you with your stopper problems.

Illinois Glass Company

Peg Stoppers

C H No. 65

C H No. 452

C H No. 254

C H No. 393

C H No. 58

C H No. 45

C H No. 348

C H No. 385

C H No. 347

Peg Stoppers

(CUTS ACTUAL SIZE)

C H No. 208

C H No. 375

C H No. 414

C H No. 252

C H No. 335

C H No. 310

C H No. 447

C H No. 330

C H No. 322

Peg Stoppers

(CUTS ACTUAL SIZE)

C H No. 423

C H No. 421

C H No. 422

C H No. 390

C H No. 420

C H No. 454

C H No. 382

C H No. 226

C H No. 225

Peg Stoppers
(CUTS ACTUAL SIZE)

C H No. 71

C H No. 260

C H No. 406

C H No. 380

C H No. 36

C H No. 379

C H No. 367

C H No. 66

C H No. 400

Peg Stoppers
(CUTS ACTUAL SIZE)

C H No. 407

C H No. 388

C H No. 387

C H No. 401

CH No. 405

C H No. 383

C H No. 334

C H No. 431

C H No. 336

Illinois Glass Company

Peg Stoppers
(CUTS ACTUAL SIZE)

C H No. 298

C H No. 465

C H No. 373

C H No. 412

C H No. 468

C H No. 463

C H No. 470

C H No. 466

C H No. 475

Illinois Glass Company

Peg Stoppers
(CUTS ACTUAL SIZE)

C H No. 37

C H No. 438

C H No. 50

C H No. 34

C H No. 399

C H No. 223

C H No. 316

C H No. 371

C H No. 394

Illinois Glass Company

Peg Stoppers
(CUTS ACTUAL SIZE)

C H No. 446

C H No. 408

C H No. 353

C H No. 291

C H No. 352

C H No. 409

C H No. 413

C H No. 7

C H No. 436

Peg Stoppers
(CUTS ACTUAL SIZE)

C H No. 32

C H No. 57

C H No. 33

C H No. 44

C H No. 303

C H No. 30

C H No. 31

C H No. 40

C H No. 378

PRICE GUIDE

All bottles are priced without labels. Original labels on bottles will bring <u>considerably</u> more.

Page 2 - $6 each

Page 3 - $3 each

Page 4 - $3 each

Page 5 - $6 each

Page 6 - $6 each

Page 7 - Top: $5
Bottom: $7

Page 8 - $5 each

Page 9 - Top: $3
Bottom: $5

Page 10 - Top Left: $5
Top Right: $5
Middle: $5
Bottom Left: $5
Bottom Right: $6

Page 11 - $5 each

Page 12 - Top Left: $5
Top Right: $3
Middle: $3
Bottom Left: $3
Bottom Right: $5

Page 13 - $5 each

Page 14 - Top Left: $6
Top Right: $10
Middle: $6
Bottom Left: $6
Bottom Right: $3

Page 15 - $6 each

Page 16 - Top Left: $5
Top Right: $10
Middle: $3
Bottom Left: $6
Bottom Right: $6

Page 17 - $6 each

Page 18 - $5 each

Page 19 - $5 each

Page 20 - $5 each

Page 21 - $5 each

Page 22 - Top Left: $3
Top Middle: $2
Top Right: $3
Middle Left: $2
Middle Mid: $4
Middle Right: $2
Bottom Left: $7
Bottom Right: $7

Page 23 - $2

Page 24 - $2 each

Page 25 - Top Mid: $8
Top Left: $2
Top Right: $2
Bot. Mid: $1
Bottom Left: $1
Bottom Right: $1

Page 26 - $1 each

Page 27 - $5 each with lid

Page 28 - Top: $3 with lid
Bottom Bottles:
$6 each (2 pc.)

Page 29 - $7 each w/stopper

Page 30 - $7 each w/stopper

Page 31 - Top Left: $4
Top Mid: $7
Top Right: $5
Mid Left: $5
Mid Right: $10
Bot Left: $3
Bot Mid: $4
Bot Right: $3

Page 32 - $4 each

Page 33 - Top Left: $6
w/stopper
Top Mid: $6
w/stopper
Top Right: $6
w/stopper
Mid Left: $4
Mid Right: $6
w/stopper
Bot Left: $3
Bot Mid: $6 w/stopper
Bot Right: $4

Page 34 - Top Left: $3
Top Mid: $3
Top Right: $3
Mid Left: $5
Mid Right: $5
Bot Left: $7w/stopper
Bot Mid: $3
Bot Rt: $8w/stopper

Page 35 - $7 each w/stopper

Page 36 - 2nd Row Mid: $6
4th Row Left: $5
Others are: $3 ea.

Page 37 - All with stoppers
Top Left: $10
Top Mid: $7
Top Right: $15
Bot Left: $7
Bot Mid: $15
Bot Right: $8

Page 38 - Top Left: $15 w/stopper
Others are: $4 ea.

Page 39 - $3 each

Page 40 - Top Left: $20
Other are: $3 ea.

Page 41 - $3 each

Page 42 - $3 each

Page 43 - $9 each
with stoppers

Page 44 - $20 each
with stoppers

Page 45 - $20 each
with stoppers

Page 46 - Top Row: $5 each
Bot Left: $8
Bot Mid: $5
Bot Right: $4

Page 47 - $5 each with lids

Page 48 - $3 each

Page 49 - All $10 ea.
w/stoppers

Page 50 - Top Row:
$10 w/stoppers
Bot Left: $6 w/stop.
Bot Mid: $3
Bot Right: $6 w/stop.

Page 51 - All $6 each with lids
Bottom Middle: $20

Page 52 - All $6 each with lids

Page 53 - All with Stoppers
Top: $10-30
Bot Left: $15-40
Bot Right: $15-30

Page 54 - All with Stoppers
Top: $10-30 w/stop.
Bot Left: $15-40
Bot Right: $15-30

Page 55 - All $30 each

Page 56 - All $40 each

Page 57 - All $25 each

Page 58 - All $15 each

Page 59 - Top: $2
Bottom: $7

Page 61 - All Stoppers $1 & up

Page 62 - All Stoppers $1 & up

Page 63 - All Stoppers $1 & up

Page 64 - All Stoppers $1 & up

Page 65 - All Stoppers $1 & up

Page 66 - All Stoppers $1 & up

Page 67 - All Stoppers $1 & up

Page 68 - All Stoppers $1 & up

Page 69 - All Stoppers $1 & up